Gabriel Koeppen

Cello Method

Have fun playing the Cello

Lesson Book 2
with online material (audio/pdf)

ED 22502D
ISMN 979-0-001-21563-3
ISBN 978-3-7957-2563-1

Revised edition 2022
with musical terms in
British and American English

SCHOTT

www.schott-music.com

Mainz · London · Madrid · Paris · New York · Tokyo · Beijing

Contents

Impressum:

Order number: ED 22502D
ISMN 979-0-001-21563-3
ISBN 978-3-7957-2563-1

Recording: Terje Grube and Markus Gierke
Violoncello and arrangements: Gabriel Koeppen

Cover photo: Monika Remus, Flensburg
Translation: Julia Rushworth
Typesetting and layout: Jan Willems, Villingen-Schwenningen
Editor: Dr Rainer Mohrs

Printed in Germany · BSS 57495

Welcome

You've learned a lot on your cello by now and can already produce some good sounds. Perhaps you've even played in a proper concert? That's a big challenge, but great fun, too.

In this book you'll find lots of new notes, rhythms and time signatures and discover new classical, folk, rock and jazz pieces. You can play almost all the pieces as a duet with your teacher or with the play-along versions.

Don't try to get by without a teacher, though!

Below many of the pieces you will find the symbol D : this means you can download additional piano accompaniments or cello parts from the Internet. On the website www.schott-music.com enter order number ED 22502D or the name of this Cello Method and select individual files from 'further information' – 'Downloads', where you can open and print them.

Here are a few tips on playing with the tracks:

1. Practise each piece without the recording first, until you feel confident.
2. If you want to play along with the play-along later, start by just listening to the piece on the recording.
3. Tune your cello carefully. Use the tuning notes on tracks 77–80 or a tuning device (A = 441).
4. Each piece has a two-measure (bar) count-in. If a piece begins with an upbeat the count-in is correspondingly shorter.
5. Almost all the pieces can be heard in two versions: once with the cello part and once without. The jam tracks are recorded without cello (apart from jam track 3).
6. Some pieces have been recorded without repeats to save time (even where a repeat is marked for playing duets).

Enjoy your practice!

Gabriel Koeppen

Please visit **www.schott-music.com/online-material** to download all audio files for free using the following voucher code:
W8CracNV

Key to symbols:

T = reference to Tune book

i = useful practice tips

L = extra tips for lessons

= writing practice

D = additional material available to download

To my fellow cello teachers

When a student is confident playing in the 1st position you can start working with this second book in my Cello Method.

The student will now learn to use extensions from 1st position and start using half position and 4th position, too. New notes and key signatures are introduced with appropriate explanations of music theory. New rhythms and time signatures appear, too, with enjoyable little writing exercises to reinforce what has been learned. Simple improvisations ('jam tracks') will also encourage composition; now and again students will need their teacher's help.

Please use this book **flexibly**:

- If a piece seems too difficult, just skip it and come back to it later.
- Half position can be introduced later on, if preferred.
- Jam tracks do not require use of new positions and finger extensions.

You can download additional piano accompaniments or cello parts for free from the Internet. Many pieces may thus be adapted for use in group tuition. In Tune Book 2 of this Cello Method you'll find a wealth of additional pieces, many of them with piano accompaniment.

Heartfelt thanks go to all the pupils and colleagues who have helped me work on this book.

I am always grateful for suggestions. I hope you will have fun working through this cello method.

Best wishes,

Gabriel Koeppen

Let's get playing:

Track 1/2 Tomorrow Morning

from Ireland
Arr.: G. K.

Backward Extensions

The interval between fingered notes is usually a half step (semitone), the smallest interval in our system of notes. The distance between open string and first finger is twice as far (a whole tone), so there is room for another note in between. In order to play that note you'll need to reach back with your index finger. Now 1st and 2nd fingers are a whole tone apart, with just a half step (semitone) between open string and 1st finger (see diagram). Don't allow the whole hand to shift with it: the other fingers and thumb stay in their original position. Don't roll the 1st finger sideways: place the fingertip on the string.

Closed

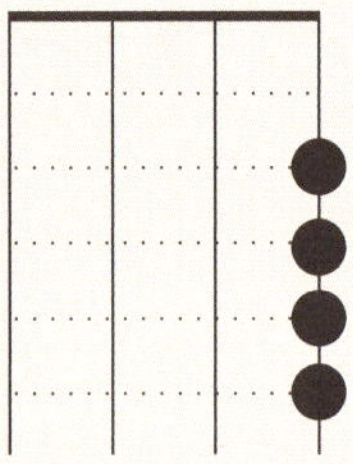

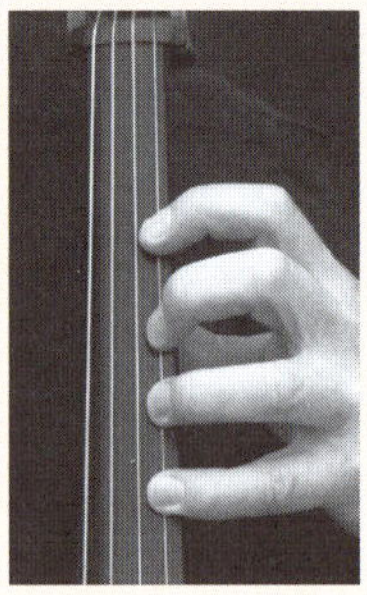

1st finger in closed position

Extended

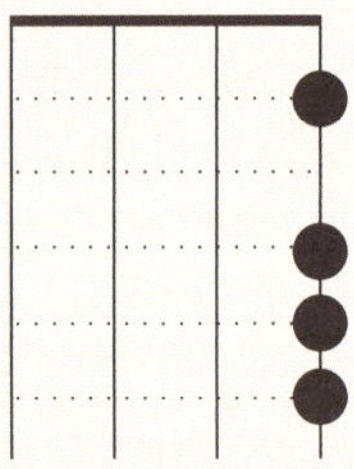

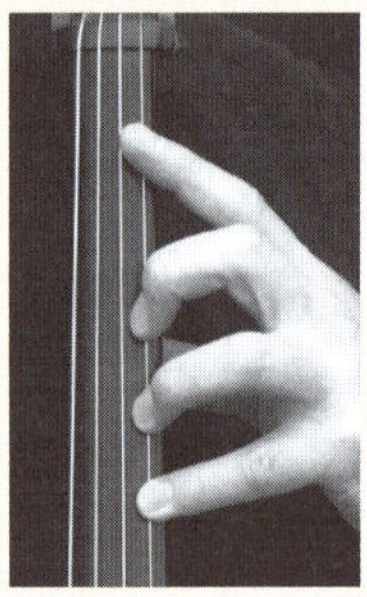

with backward extension

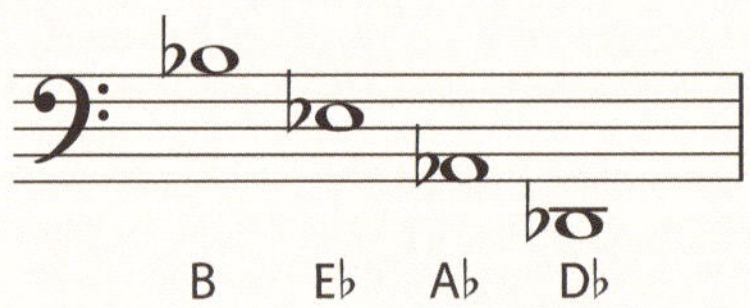

Exercises on the A string

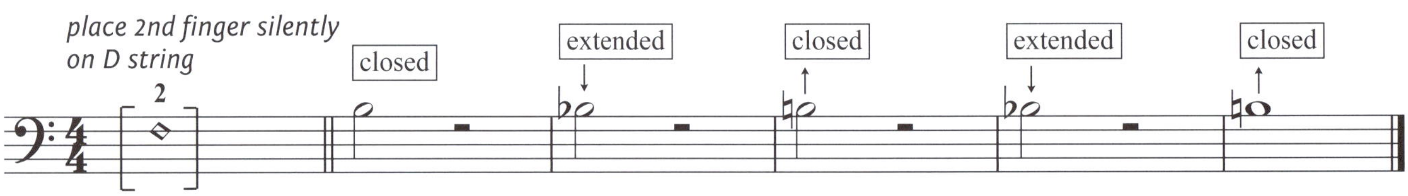

¢ = 2/2 Unlike 4/4 time, **2/2** time (Italian: *alla breve*) is counted in half notes (minims). This time signature often indicates a quick tempo.

Track 3/4

Branle

In this piece the 1st finger is always extended backwards on the A string

c. 1560

Piano part

Track 5/6

Long, long ago

Traditional
Arr.: Gabriel Koeppen

Use extended position

Try starting this tune on a lower string, using 2nd finger on the G string.
Can you write this version down? You'll find manuscript paper at the end of this book.

Piano part

Exercise on the D string

B♭ major scale

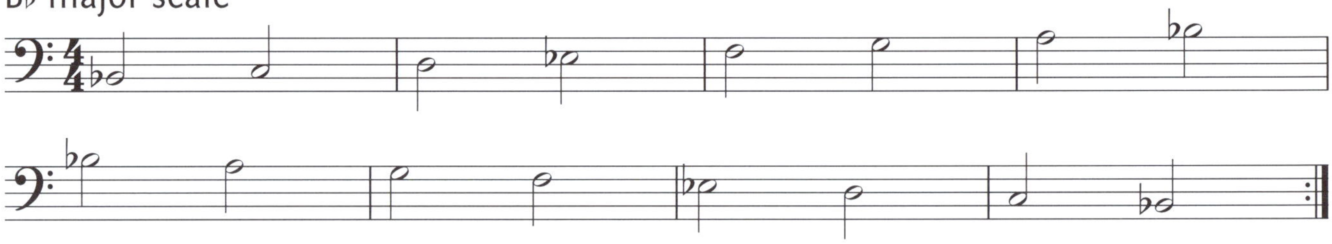

B♭ major broken chord

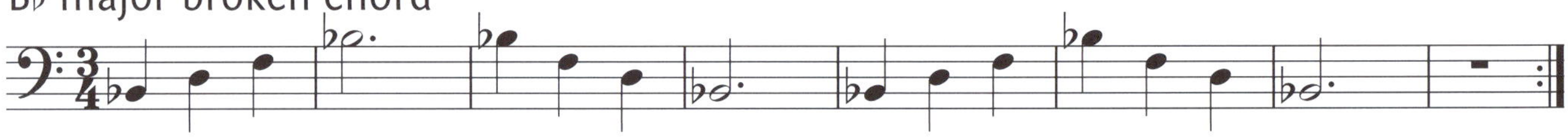

i try the bowing patterns at the back of this book, too

Track 7/8

Dance tune

Melchior Franck
(1580–1639)
Arr.: G. K.

D Piano part

Track 9/10

Rodeo

Check the key signature!

G. Koeppen

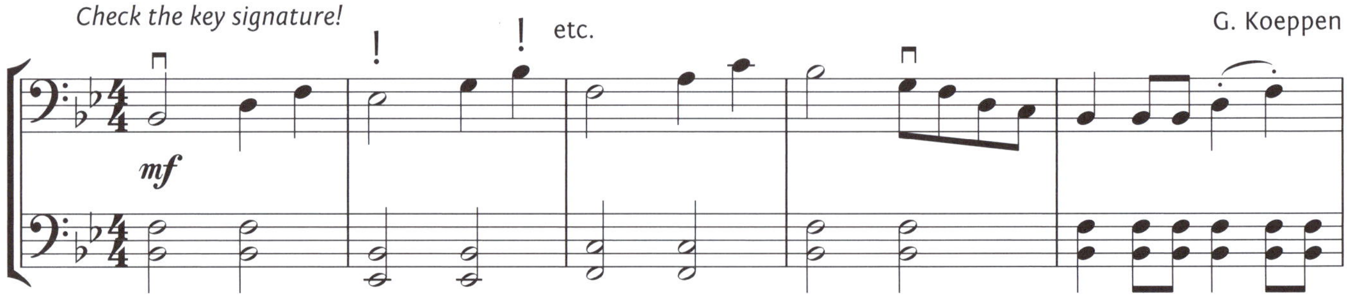

From: G. Koeppen, Nette Duette (Duets for Fun), Schott ED 21395

Piano part
additional cello parts

Gavotte

Arr.: E. Doflein

Exercise on the G string

Prélude

Jacques-Martin Hotteterre
(1674–1763)

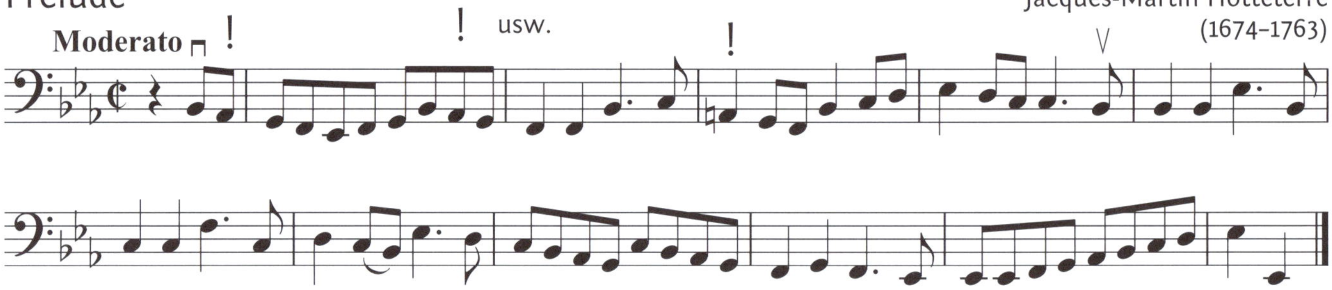

Exercise on the C string

Track 11/12 **Rockin' Bass**

G. K.

Note quiz

Write in the note names:

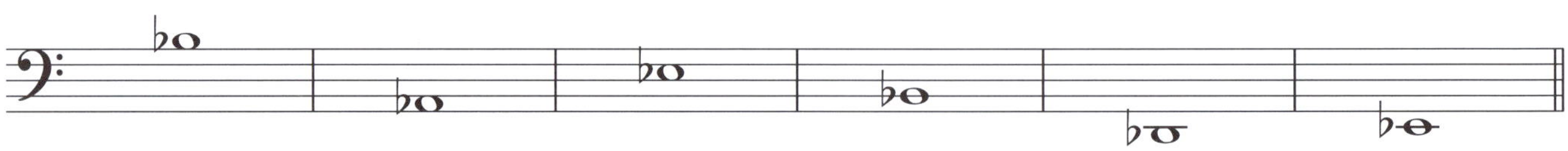

________ ________ ________ ________ ________ ________

Bridal Song (R. Schumann) and other pieces

Sixteenth notes (semiquavers)

A sixteenth note (semiquaver) sounds half as long as a eighth note (quaver). Individual sixteenth notes (semiquavers) have double flags. As with eighth notes (quavers), groups of sixteenth notes (semiquavers) are joined with beams.

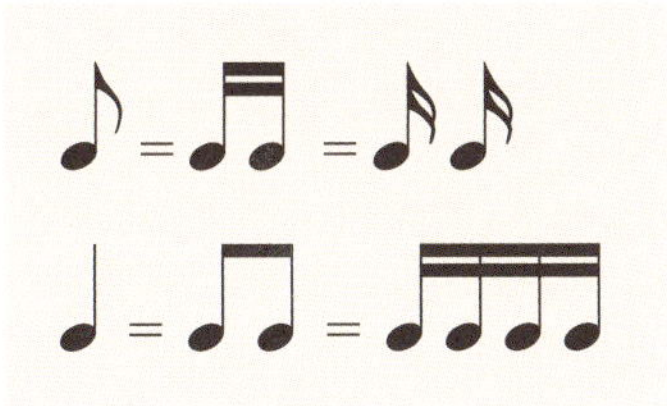

Exercises

Tap the following rhythms (on the edge of a table or on the body of the cello) before playing them with the bow.

Write a rhythmic duet using one or several notes:

Clock Canon

Traditional
English text: Julia Rushworth

Play the Clock Canon on a lower string:
start with your 4th finger on the C string.

2/4 Only 2 quarter notes (crotchets) fit into a 2/4 bar.
Now every second quarter note (crotchet) is accented.

Track 13/14 Old Brass Wagon

traditional
Arr.: Gabriel Koeppen

Try playing this tune starting with your 4th finger on the G string, too.
Can you write this version down?

D Piano part

Track 15/16 Breakout

G. K.

Accompaniment: 2nd Vc unisono, playing an octave higher ad lib.

You already know this tune from Book 1. I wanted to try playing it faster,
so I just wrote shorter note values. I've left out a few beams, though: can you mark them in?

What shall we do

Traditional

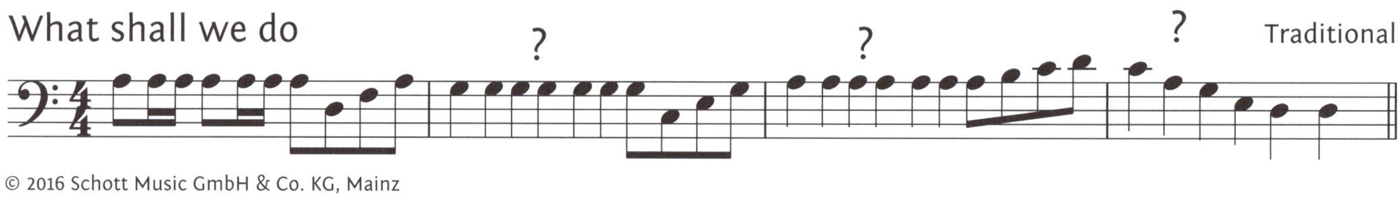

Track 17/18 Skip To My Lou

Traditional
Arr.: Gabriel Koeppen

recording: without repeat

D Piano part

Theme from the overture to 'William Tell'

Gioachino Antonio Rossini
(1792–1868)
Arr.: G. K.

Learn the 2nd part first

Allegro

A Jolly Outing

Fill in the names and write in the rhythms. Make up a melody to fit the rhythm and write it on the stave.

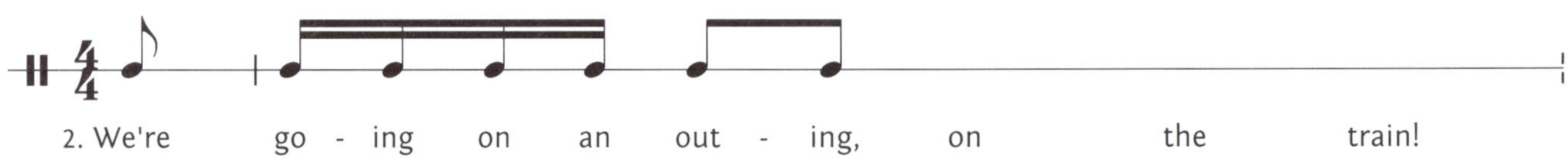

Write the rhythm that fits the words:

________________, ________________, ________________, ________________:

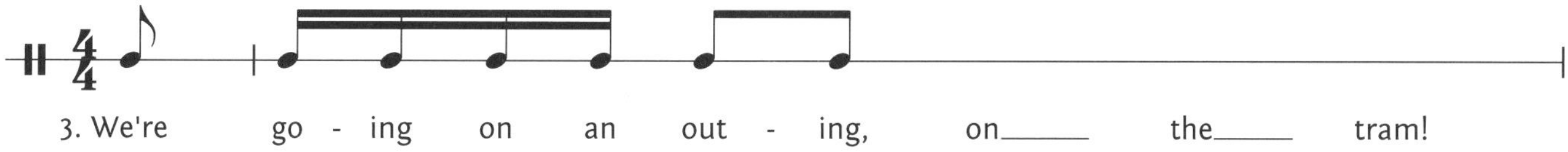

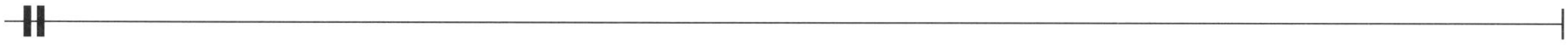

______, ______, ______, ______:

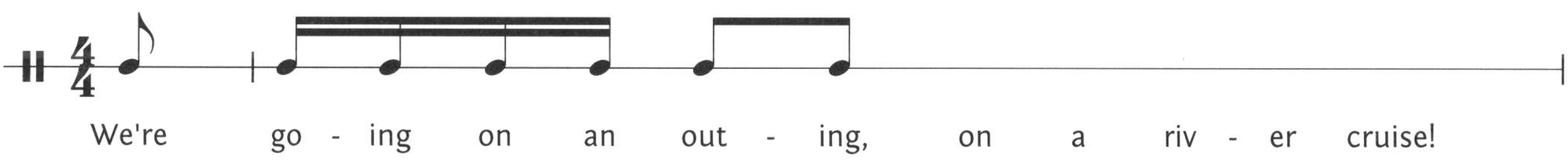

______, ______, ______, ______:

Here are some examples of names set as rhythms. Can you think of others?

 Jane, John, Kim, Tim, Bob, Clare, ______

 Alex, Tony, Astrid, Peter, ______

 Jennifer, William, ______

 Isabella, Alexander, Henrietta, Valentino, ______

Track 19 Jam track 1: Meditation

Carry on playing with these notes:

D minor pentatonic (5-note scale)

Write a piece and play it along with the jam track:

Name of the piece ______________________ Composer ______________________

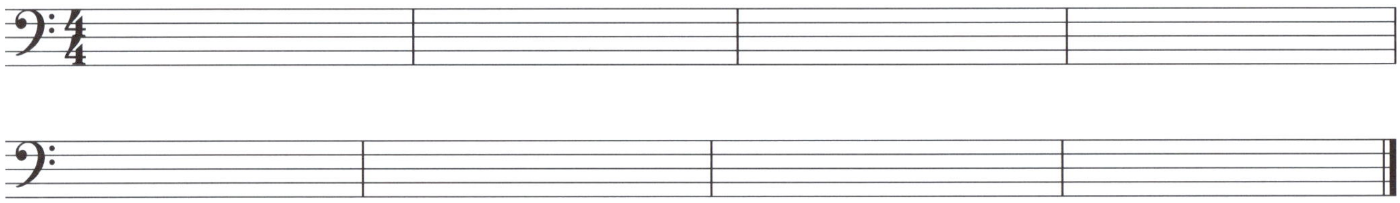

Accompaniment:

vary the accompaniment *ad lib.*

A Merry Chase

Player 1 decides when the notes will change, player 2 has to follow.
Start with long notes. Watch each other at first, then try without looking.

Level 1 (easy): the order is fixed, for example player 1 plays the C major scale:

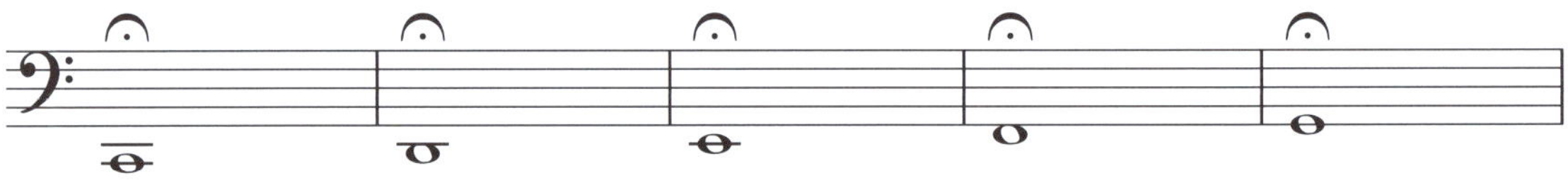

etc.

Level 2 (harder): notes only move in small steps,
but may change direction ('snake pattern'), for example:

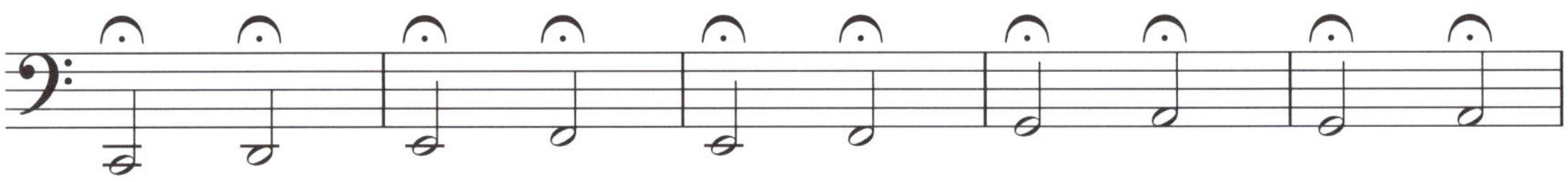

etc.

Level 3 (hard): jump across any intervals in both directions, for example:

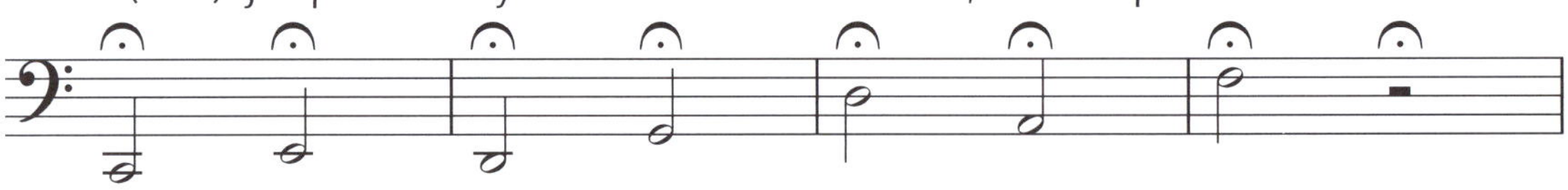

etc.

Musette

From 'Wolfgang's music book'

Leopold Mozart
(1719–1797)
Arr.: G. K.

Counting exercises:

How many sixteenths (semiquavers) will match these notes?

Add them together:

Forward Extensions

With a forward extension you can reach another note with the 4th finger. The hand shifts up a half step (semitone) towards the bridge, while the 1st finger reaches back and stays in the same place as before in 1st position. Now there is a whole tone between open string and 1st finger and between 1st and 2nd finger, too.

Close

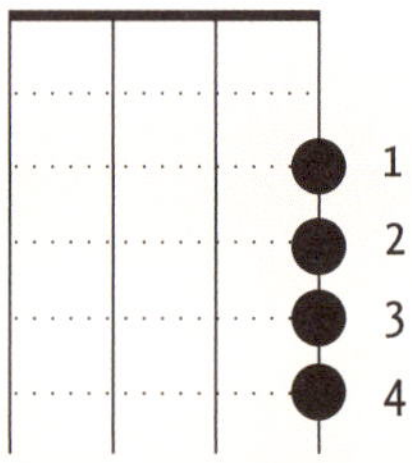

4th finger in closed position

Extended

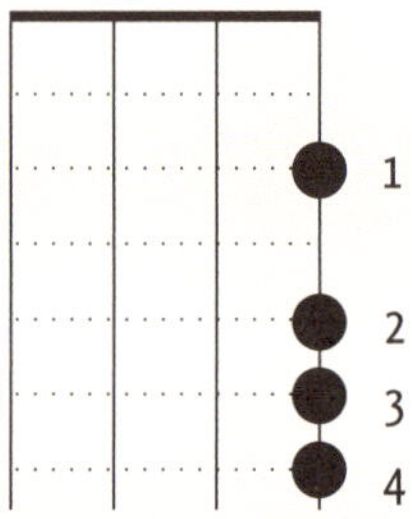

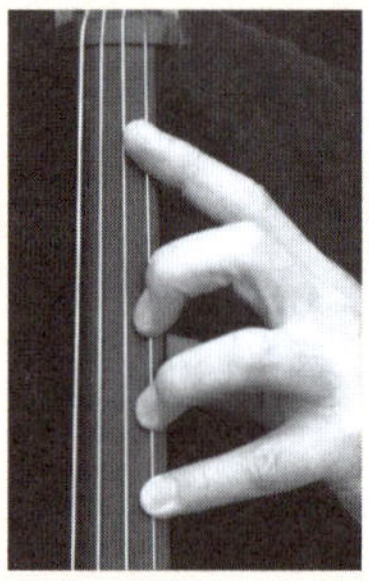

4th finger in forward extension

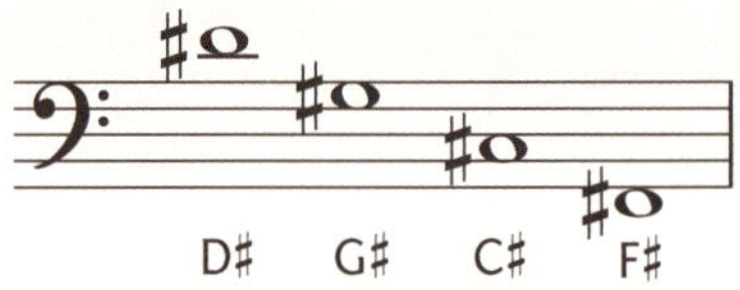

Find the notes

An old favourite:

Merrily We Roll Along

Play by heart: 'O when the Saints'.
Start with the 1st finger on the D string.

Track 20/21 Alouette

French folksong
Arr.: G. K.

D. C. al Fine

Try playing 'Alouette' with backward extension, too. Can you write it down?

D Piano part

Find the notes on the G string

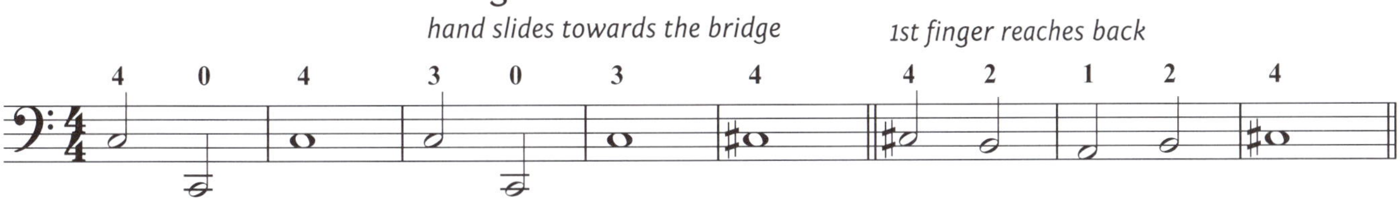

Play 'Merrily We Roll Along' on the G string, starting on C♯.

Goblins' Dance

G. K.

Try playing the Goblins' Dance on the D string.
What accidentals do you need?

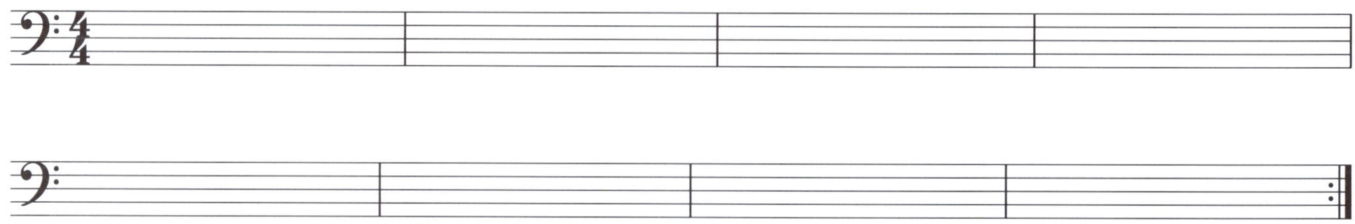

Track 22/23

Allemande

Tilman Susato
(1510–1570)
Arr.: G. K.

D Piano part

A major scale

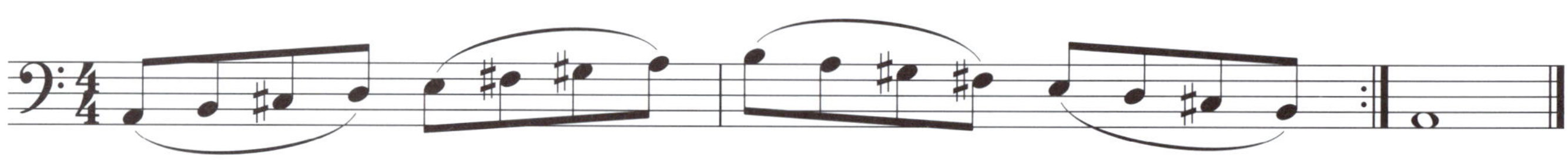

A major broken chord

Other bowings are shown at the back of this book.

Track 32/33 Yankee Doodle

Traditional
Arr.: G. K.

D Piano part

Spoken Trio

G. K.

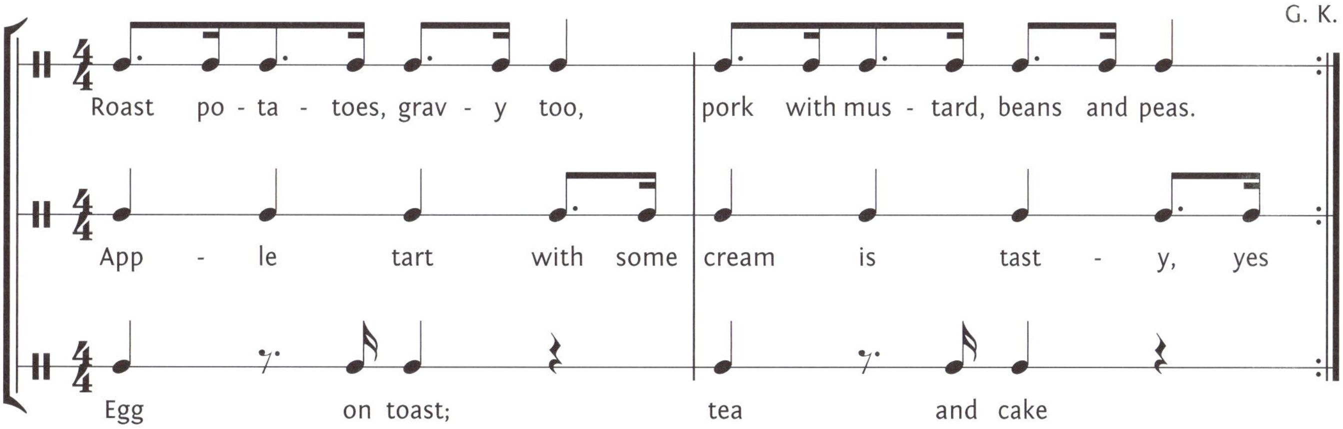

These rhythms can also (or alternatively) be tapped out with different sounds. For instance: 1st part – rub hands together or against the body of the cello, 2nd part – tap the side of the cello, 3rd part – stamp your foot or knock the back of the cello. This works as a duet, too, of course. It can be fun to swap parts suddenly!

If a dotted rhythm is not to sound *legato* it makes bowing a bit more difficult. In practice, the dotted note is often shortened. It's easier to bow two notes in the same direction:

Track 34/35 **If You're Happy And You Know It**

Traditional
Arr.: G. Koeppen

*) stamp your feet

D Piano part

T Auld Lang Syne and other pieces

A **grace note** (written smaller) is played just before the main note and is usually slurred. If there is a line through the stem, the grace note is played short (like a sixteenth/semiquaver).

Grazioso

Jean Baptiste Bréval
(1753–1823)

from: Jean Baptiste Bréval, Easy pieces for 2 Cellos, Book 2, Schott ED 6159

Enharmonic Equivalents

The black key between D and E on the piano can be reached by sharpening the D or flattening the E, so the same note has two different names: DK or EL. This is called an enharmonic equivalent.

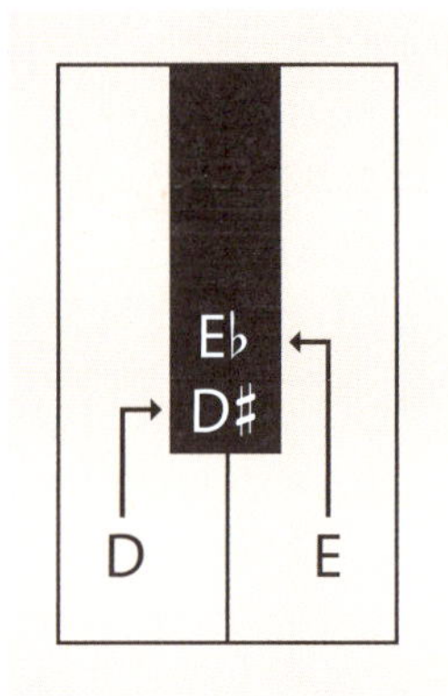

If a note is raised with a ♯ we add the word 'sharp' to its name, for example: F sharp, C sharp, G sharp or D sharp (F♯, C♯, G♯, D♯). If a note is lowered with a ♭ we add the word 'flat' to its name, for example: E flat, A flat, D flat or B flat (E♭, A♭, D♭, B♭).

These are the most common 'enharmonic equivalents':

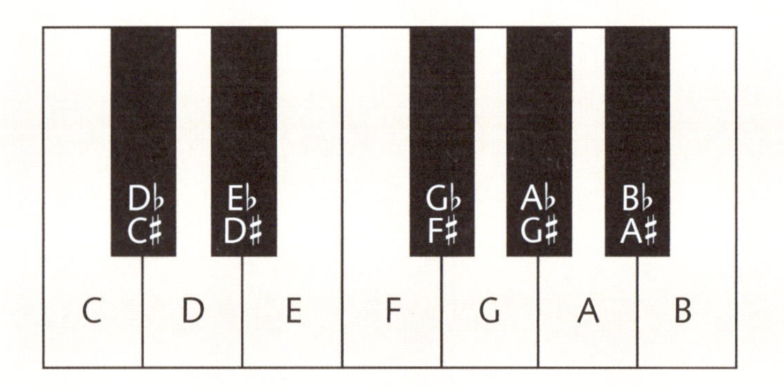

Even white keys on a keyboard can have names for enharmonic equivalents

Find a few enharmonic equivalents:

The Puzzled Pharaoh

Use downward extended position

G. K.

Make up your own accompaniment.

Half Position

You'll find half position if you slide your whole hand down by a half step (semitone) from 1st position (towards the nut).

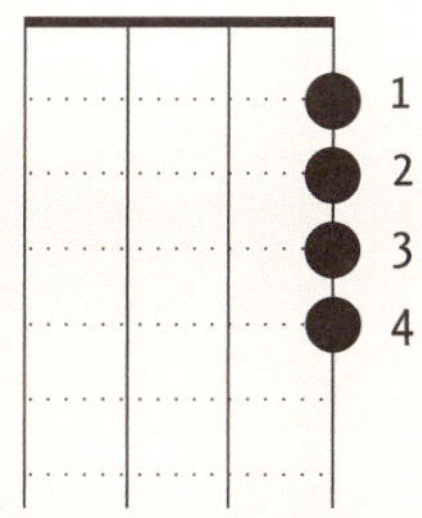

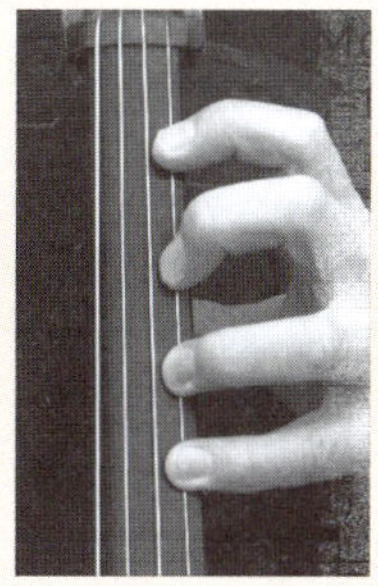

Exercises

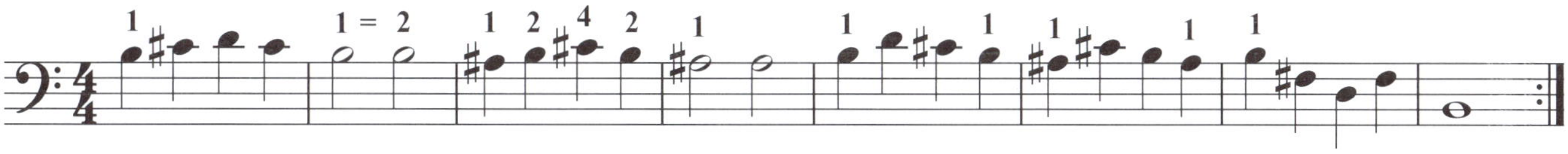

Write in the fingering

Are there other possibilities?

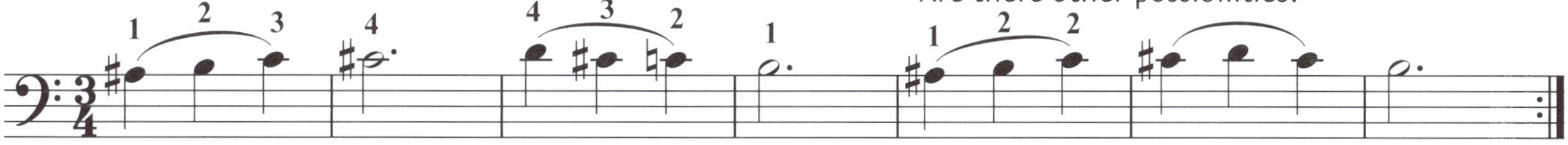

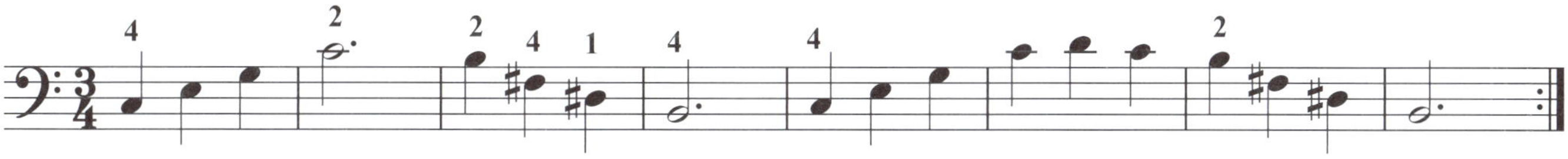

Study in E minor

Sebastian Lee (1805–1887)

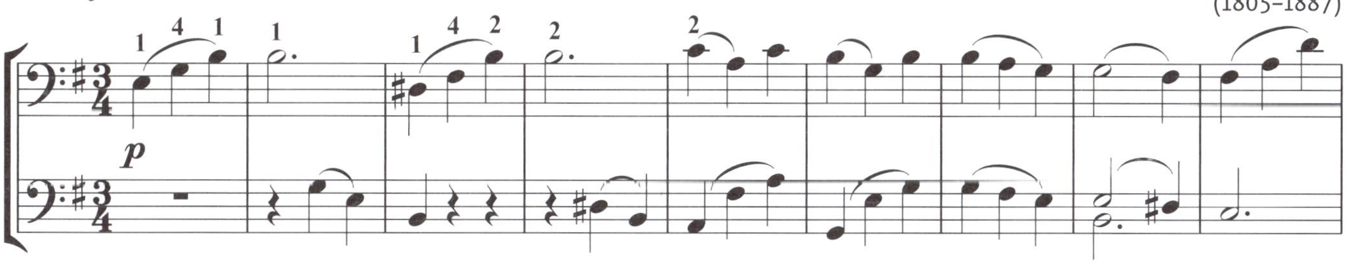

Track 36/37

Fate

G. K.

Space for your own notes, exercises or composition

March of the Toreadors (G. Bizet) and other pieces

6/8 Time

Hang on, isn't 6/8 the same as 3/4?
The difference is in the accented beats, shown by grouping with beams, for example:

3/4 time: 

6/8 time: 

Evening Canon

Traditional

Jig

from Crome
2nd part by G. K.

Track 38/39 Skye Boat Song

from Scotland
Arr.: G. Koeppen

Slow and sustained

D
Piano part
additional cello part

Track 32/33

Yankee Doodle

Traditional
Arr.: G. K.

D Piano part

Spoken Trio

G. K.

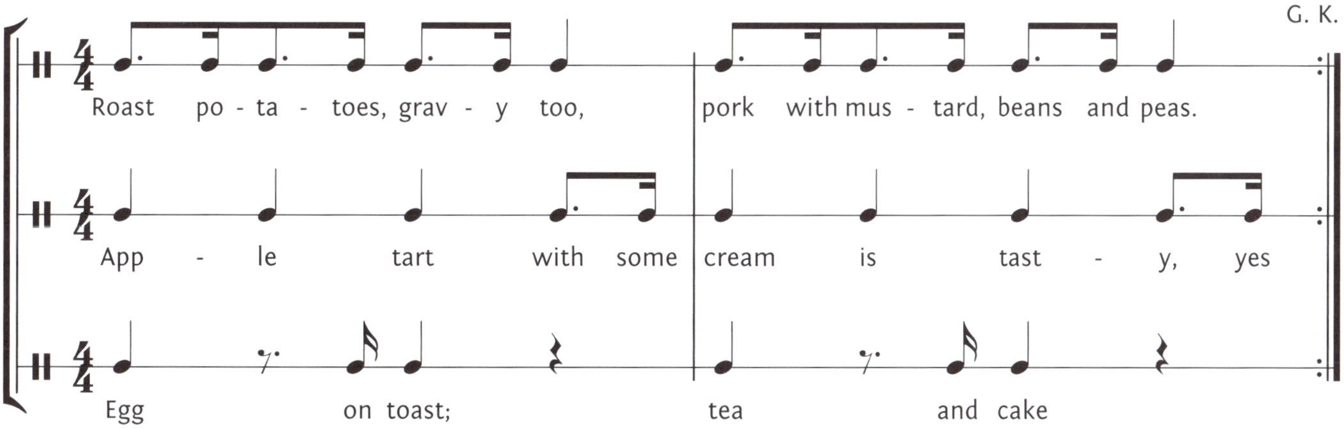

These rhythms can also (or alternatively) be tapped out with different sounds. For instance: 1st part – rub hands together or against the body of the cello, 2nd part – tap the side of the cello, 3rd part – stamp your foot or knock the back of the cello. This works as a duet, too, of course. It can be fun to swap parts suddenly!

If a dotted rhythm is not to sound *legato* it makes bowing a bit more difficult. In practice, the dotted note is often shortened. It's easier to bow two notes in the same direction:

Track 34/35 **If You're Happy And You Know It**

Traditional
Arr.: G. Koeppen

*) stamp your feet

D Piano part

T Auld Lang Syne and other pieces

A **grace note** (written smaller) is played just before the main note and is usually slurred. If there is a line through the stem, the grace note is played short (like a sixteenth/semiquaver).

Grazioso

Jean Baptiste Bréval
(1753–1823)

from: Jean Baptiste Bréval, Easy pieces for 2 Cellos, Book 2, Schott ED 6159

Enharmonic Equivalents

The black key between D and E on the piano can be reached by sharpening the D or flattening the E, so the same note has two different names: DK or EL. This is called an enharmonic equivalent.

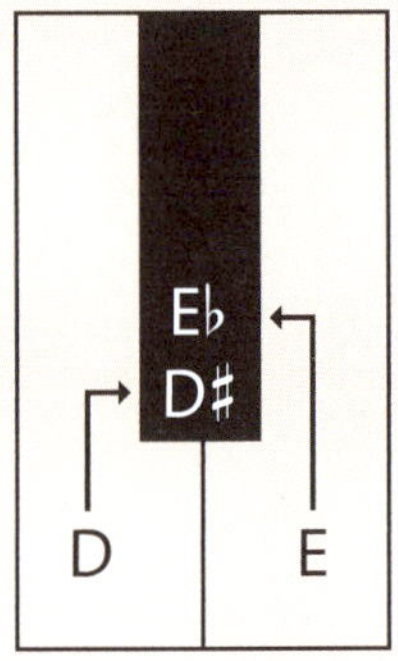

If a note is raised with a ♯ we add the word 'sharp' to its name, for example: F sharp, C sharp, G sharp or D sharp (F♯, C♯, G♯, D♯). If a note is lowered with a ♭ we add the word 'flat' to its name, for example: E flat, A flat, D flat or B flat (E♭, A♭, D♭, B♭).

These are the most common 'enharmonic equivalents':

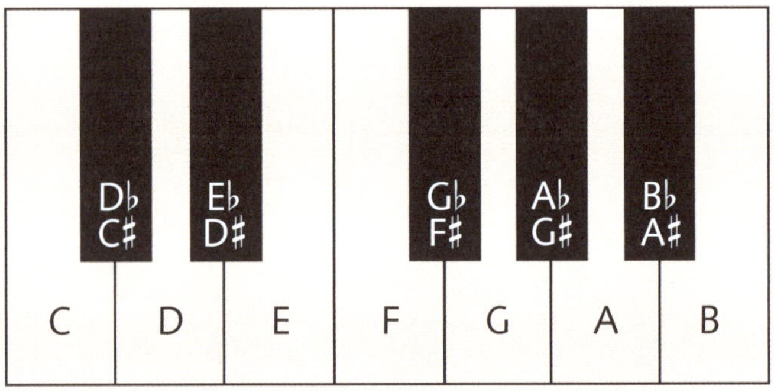

Even white keys on a keyboard can have names for enharmonic equivalents

Find a few enharmonic equivalents:

The Puzzled Pharaoh

Use downward extended position

G. K.

Make up your own accompaniment.

Half Position

You'll find half position if you slide your whole hand down by a half step (semitone) from 1st position (towards the nut).

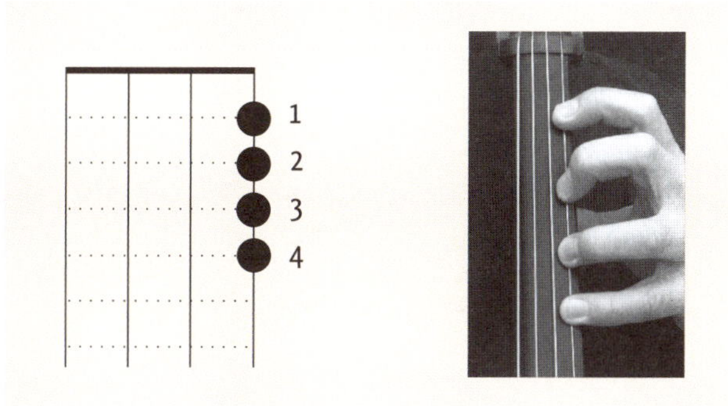

Exercises

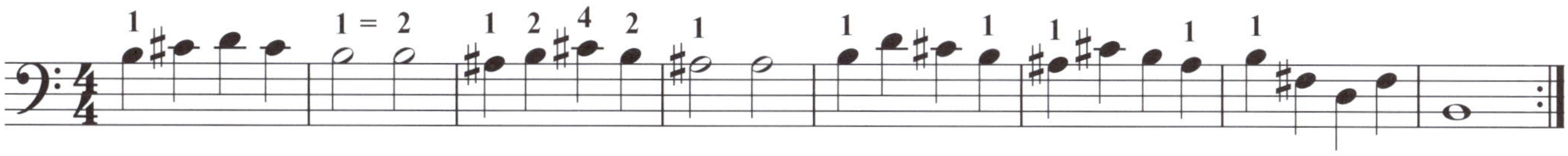

Write in the fingering

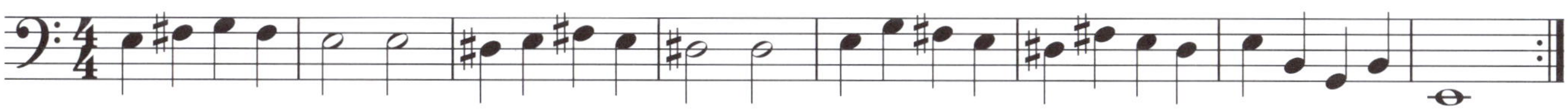

Are there other possibilities?

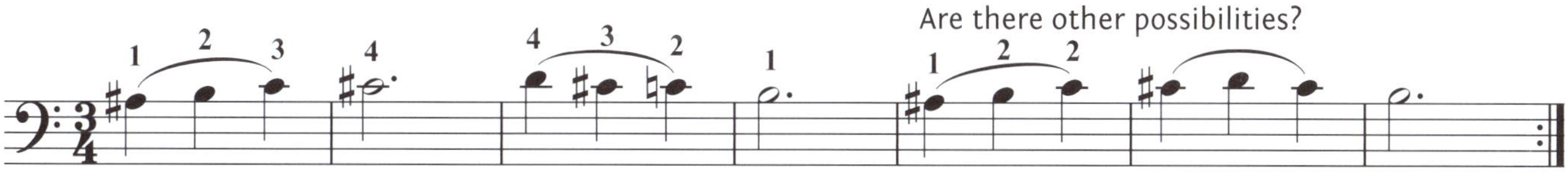

Study in E minor

Sebastian Lee
(1805–1887)

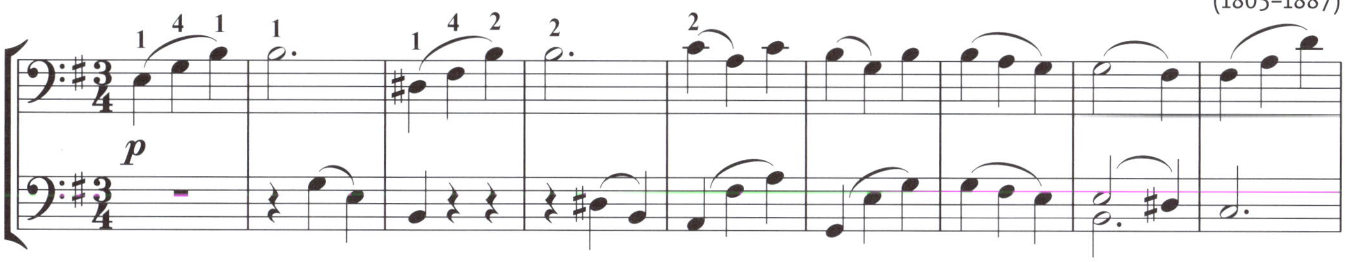

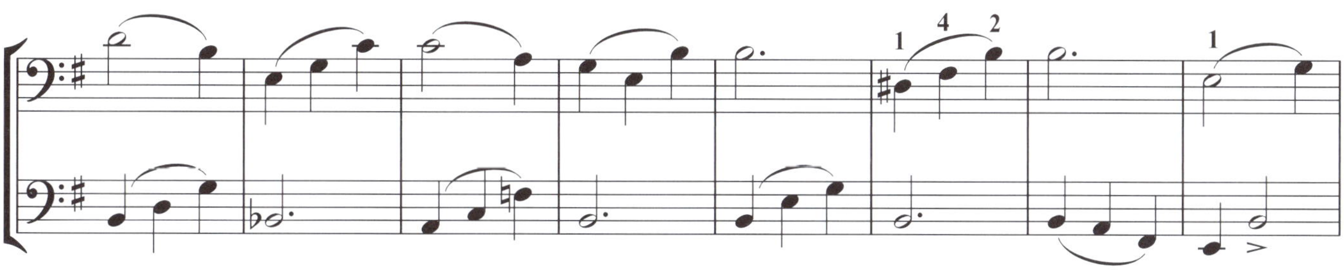

Track 36/37 **Fate**

G. K.

Space for your own notes, exercises or composition

March of the Toreadors (G. Bizet) and other pieces

6/8 Time

Hang on, isn't 6/8 the same as 3/4?
The difference is in the accented beats, shown by grouping with beams, for example:

Evening Canon

Traditional

Jig

from Crome
2nd part by G. K.

Track 38/39

Skye Boat Song

from Scotland
Arr.: G. Koeppen

D
Piano part
additional cello part

Track 40/41 Jazzy Tarantella

Lively G. K.

D Piano part
additional cello parts

Work out the time signature and write it in:

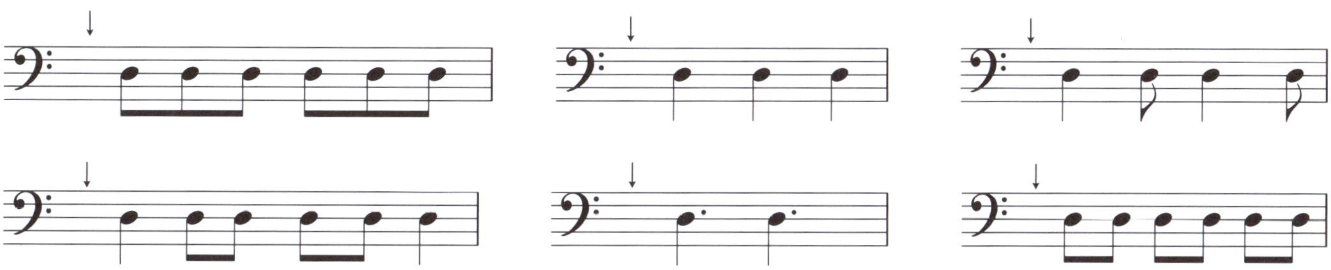

The next tune uses both kinds of extended position:

Track 42/43 **Greensleeves**

Traditional
Arr.: G. K.

D Piano part

T Andante Grazioso (W. A. Mozart) and other pieces

Track 44 Playing by ear

Now I'll play you some little sequences of notes on the A string: listen to the recording. I'll tell you the first note. Try to play the same notes by heart and write them down. These notes are used:

Here comes one more note:

Track 45

The second aural test can be done later on if you like.

Track 46 Jam Track 2: Billy's Rock

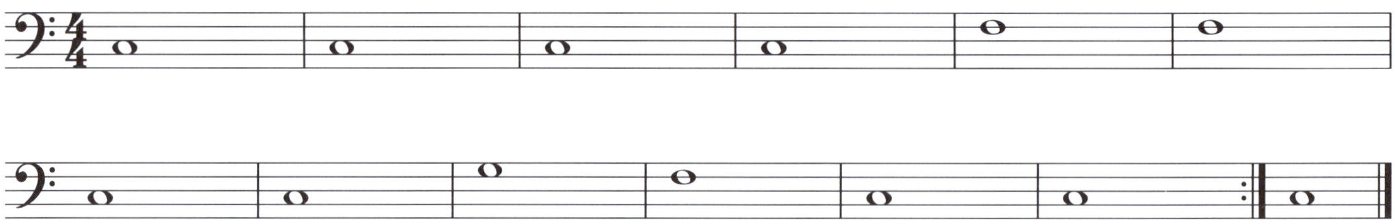

Fill each whole note (semibreve) with your own rhythms, for example:

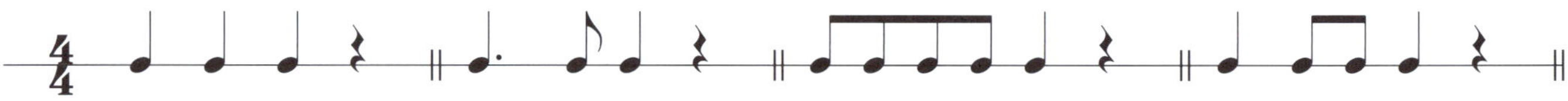

Use your own rhythms:

Write your own piece using the same note changes:

Name of the piece

Composer

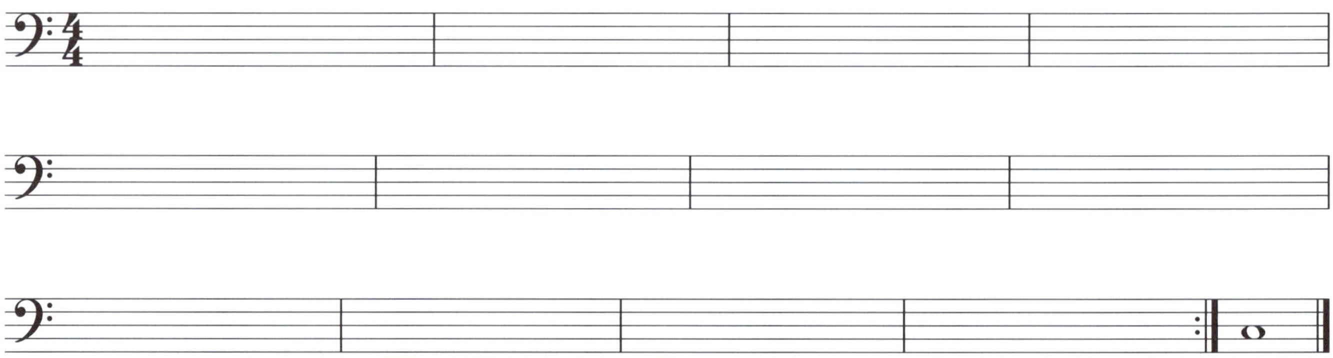

Accompaniment

D 'Professional' version with chords

Running and Jumping

Study in playing fast

G. K.

4th Position

If you slide your hand along the fingerboard further towards the bridge, you can play even higher notes. This often makes it possible to play sequences of notes more smoothly. Melodies often flow better when you use string changes. Now you can play several notes on two different strings. In a higher position the notes sound softer and you can avoid open strings, which sometimes don't sound good.
We'll start with 4th position. This is particularly easy to find, because the thumb rests in the crook of the neck.

The thumb rests in crook of neck:

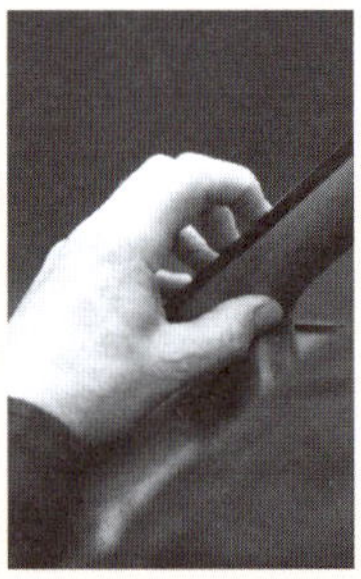

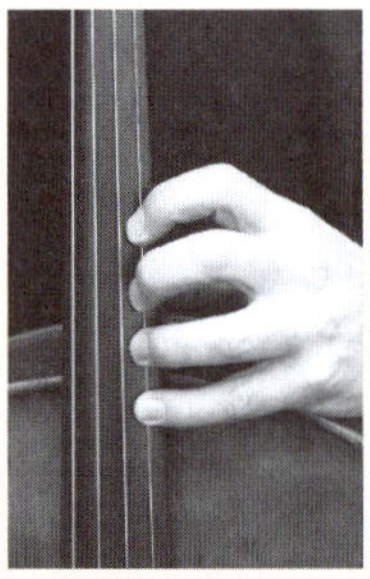

Fingers are closer together in 4th position.

Find the notes

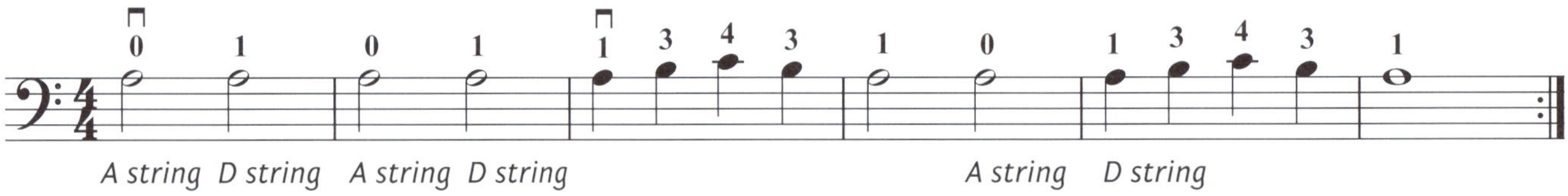

Little Duet

In 4th position on the D string

G. K.

Find the notes

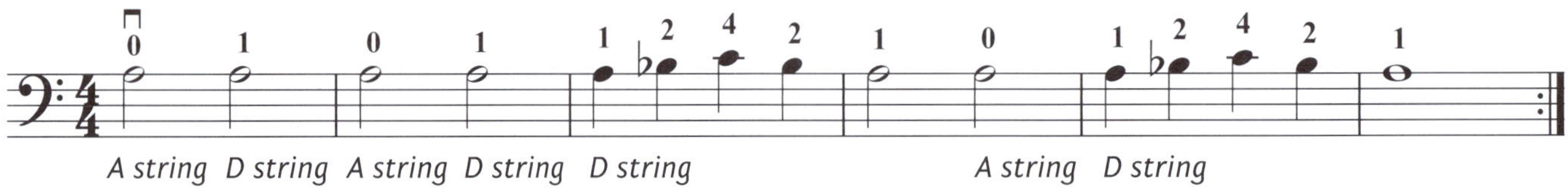

Bavarian Rag

G. K.

Find the notes

Place 1st finger on the A string

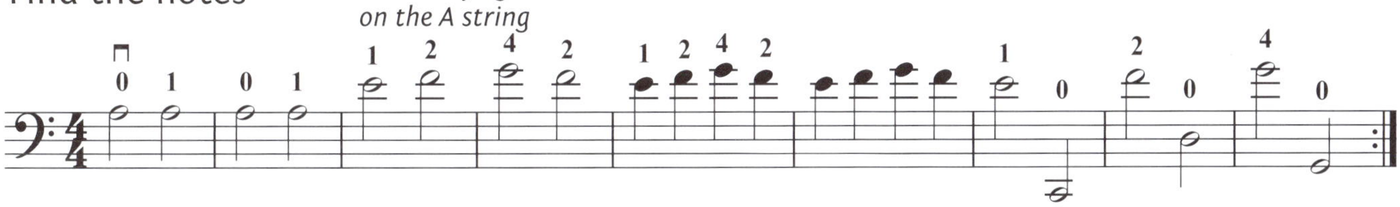

Track 47/48

Rock It!

G. K.

Find the notes

Flowing

G. K.

Searching

on A and D strings

G. K.

Track 40/41 Jazzy Tarantella

D Piano part
additional cello parts

Work out the time signature and write it in:

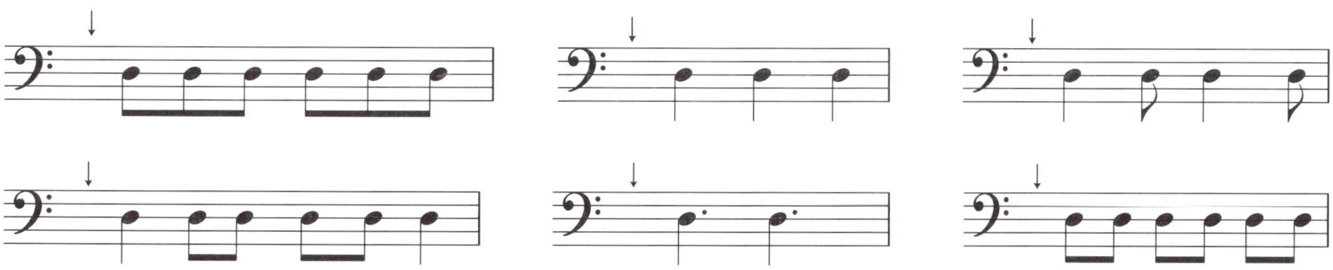

The next tune uses both kinds of extended position:

Track 42/43 **Greensleeves**

Traditional
Arr.: G. K.

D Piano part

T Andante Grazioso (W. A. Mozart) and other pieces

Track 44

Playing by ear

Now I'll play you some little sequences of notes on the A string: listen to the recording. I'll tell you the first note. Try to play the same notes by heart and write them down. These notes are used:

Here comes one more note:

Track 45

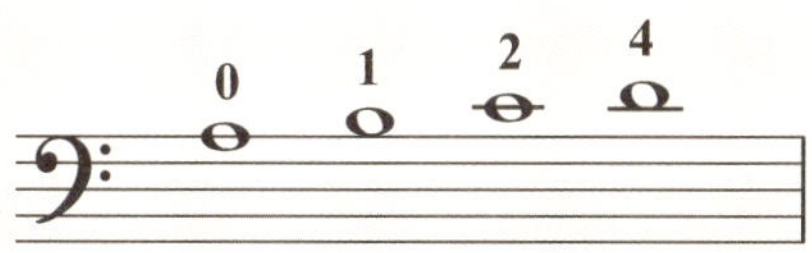

The second aural test can be done later on if you like.

Track 46 Jam Track 2: Billy's Rock

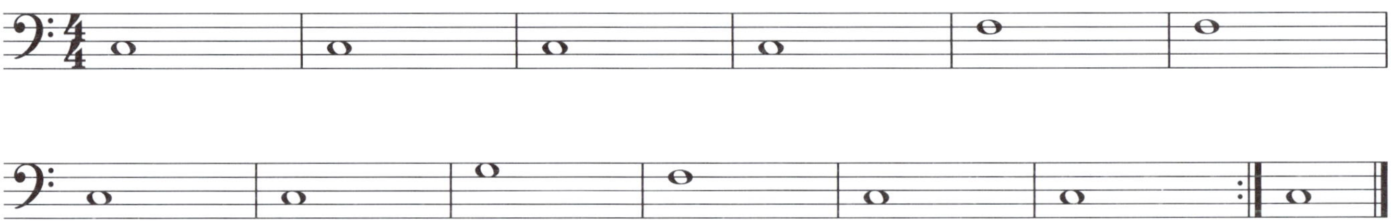

Fill each whole note (semibreve) with your own rhythms, for example:

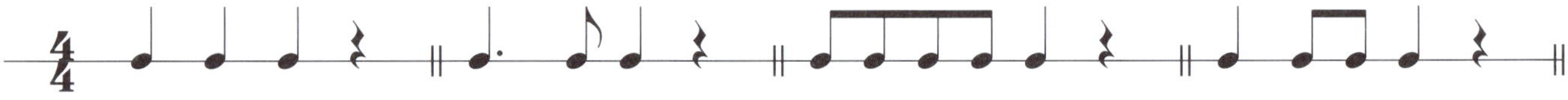

Use your own rhythms:

Write your own piece using the same note changes:

Name of the piece ____________________ Composer ____________________

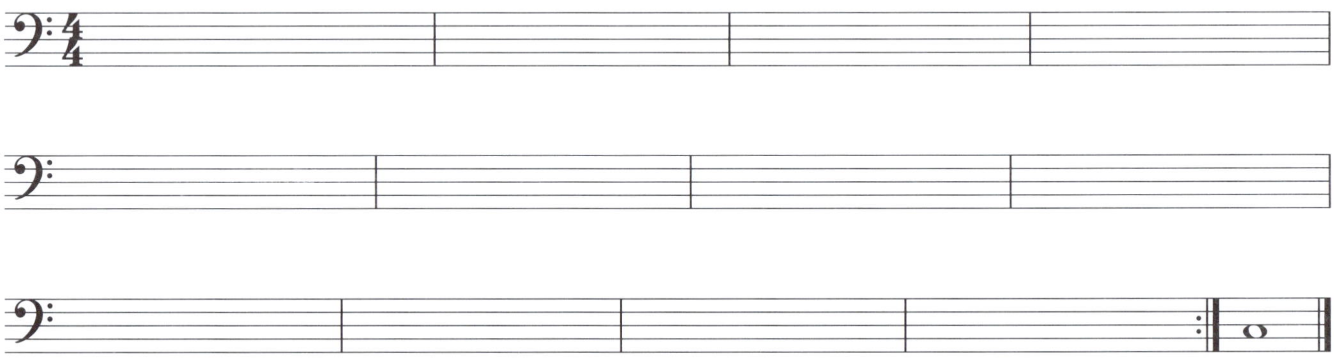

Accompaniment

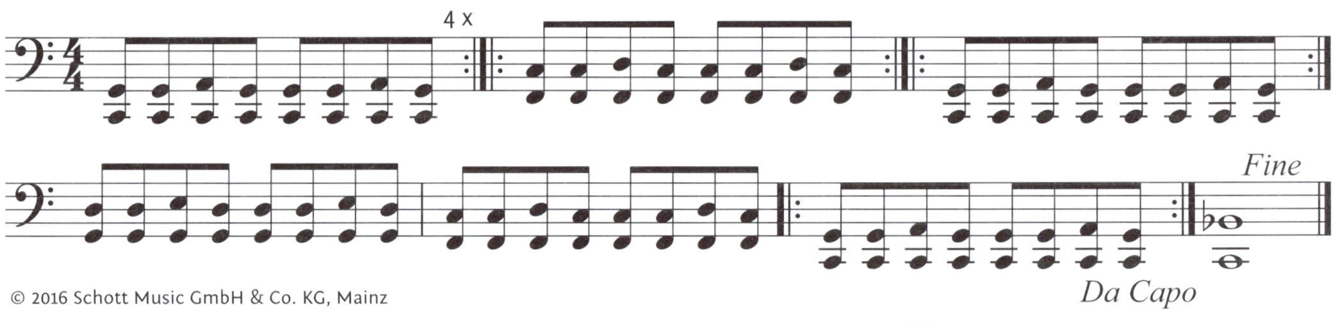

D 'Professional' version with chords

Running and Jumping

Study in playing fast

Allegro G. K.

4th Position

If you slide your hand along the fingerboard further towards the bridge, you can play even higher notes. This often makes it possible to play sequences of notes more smoothly. Melodies often flow better when you use string changes. Now you can play several notes on two different strings. In a higher position the notes sound softer and you can avoid open strings, which sometimes don't sound good.
We'll start with 4th position. This is particularly easy to find, because the thumb rests in the crook of the neck.

The thumb rests in crook of neck:

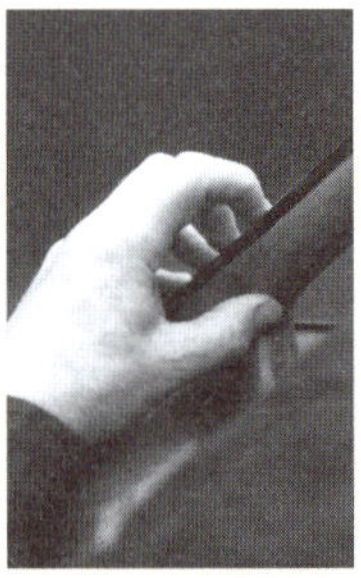

Fingers are closer together in 4th position.

Find the notes

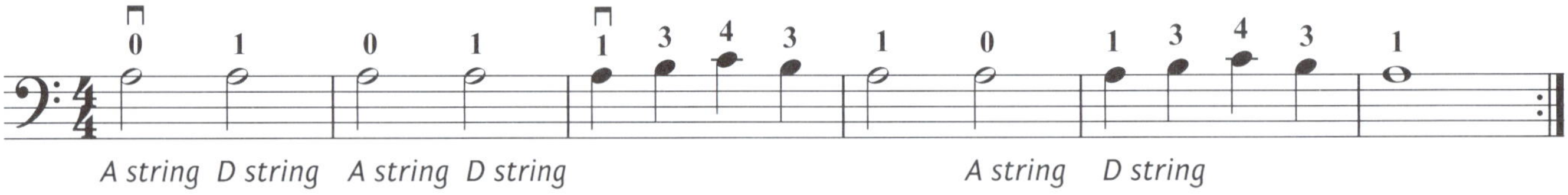

Little Duet

In 4th position on the D string

G. K.

Find the notes

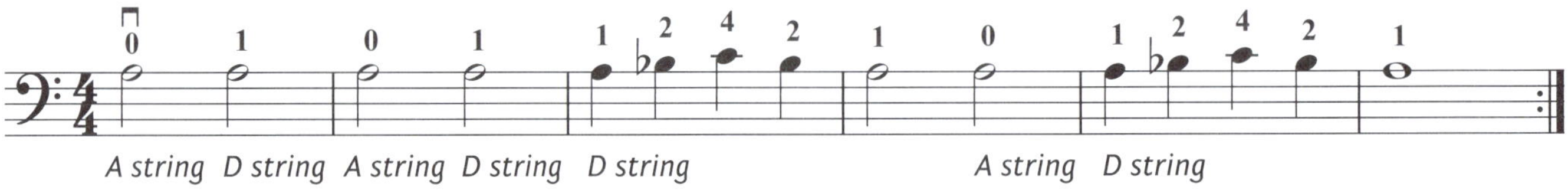

Bavarian Rag

G. K.

Find the notes

Place 1st finger on the A string

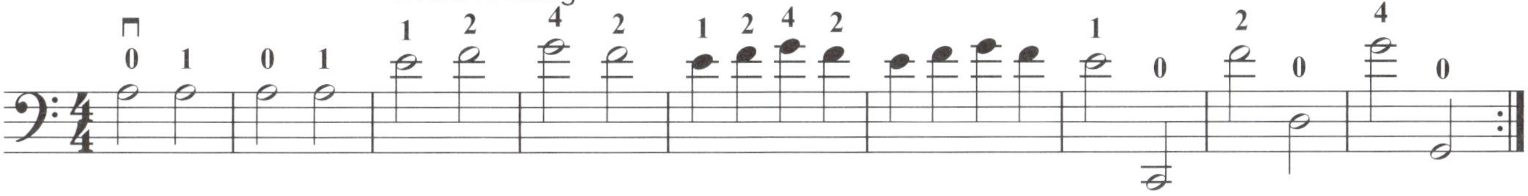

Track 47/48

Rock It!

G. K.

Find the notes

Flowing

G. K.

Searching

on A and D strings

G. K.

Theme with Variations

Theme

G. K.

finish writing the variations:

Variation 1

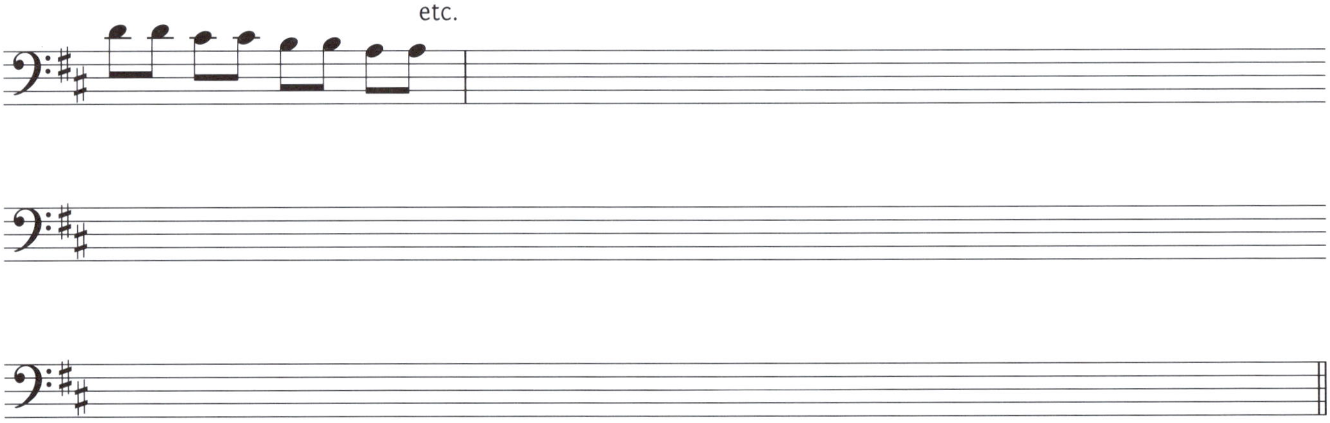

Variation 2

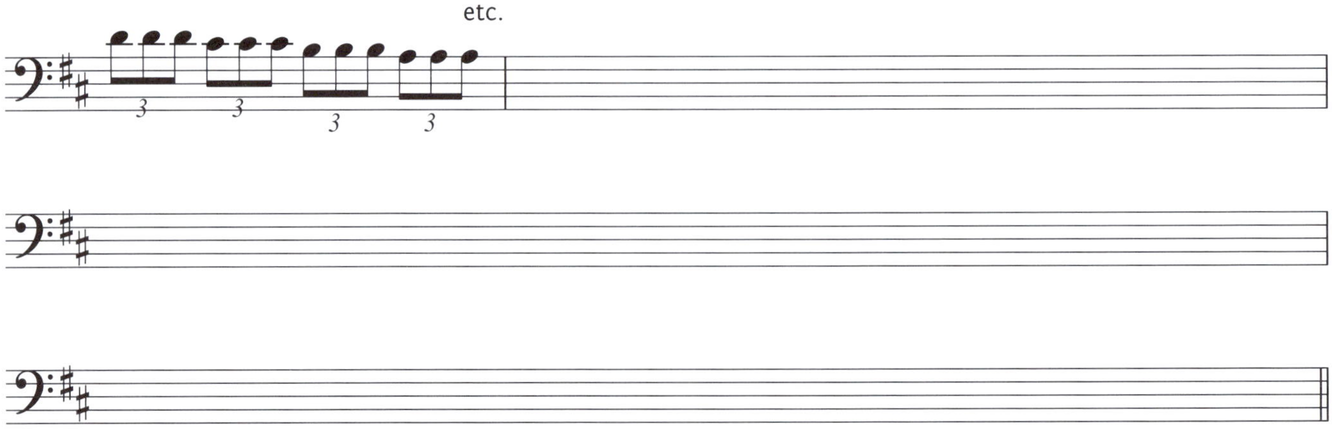

Variation 3

Write a few freer variations on the theme. Try different rhythms, include rests, change the key, jump around or try a different time signature.

Variation 4

Variation 5

The accompaniment can be varied too, to go with different variations.

Position Changes

Change from 1st position to 4th position and back again

During the rest, slide the 1st finger into 4th position (don't jump).

D string

A string

During the rest, the 1st finger takes over again.

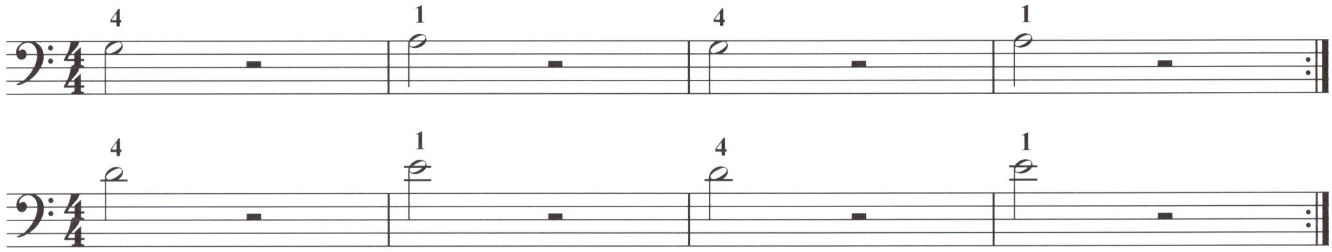

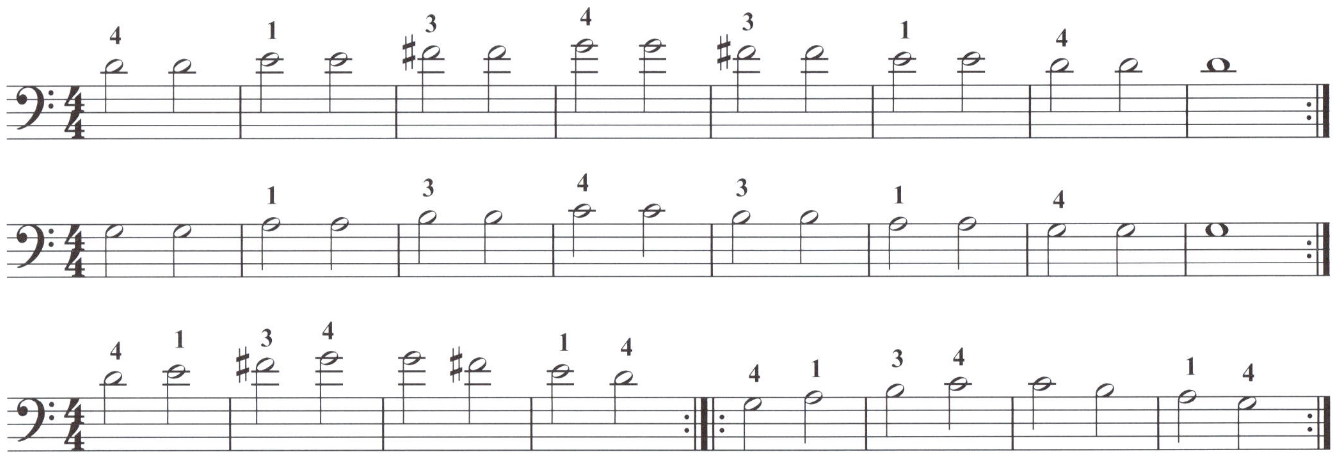

Now you can play the G major scale over two octaves:

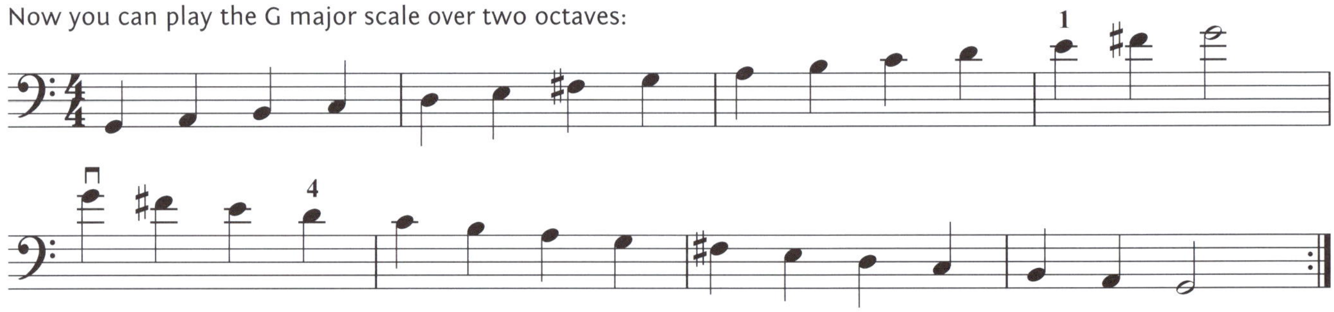

And the broken chord that goes with it:

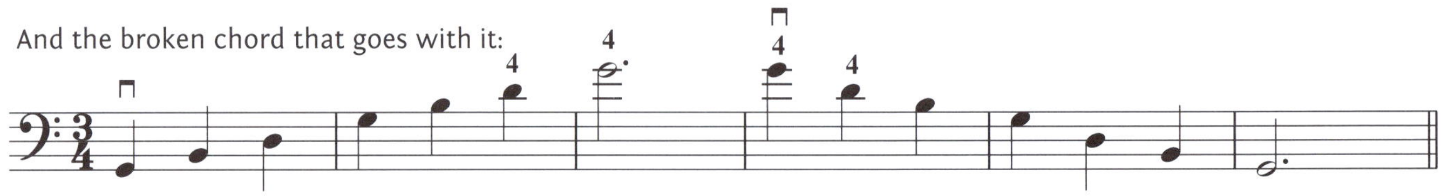

There are other bowing patterns at the back of this book.

Hungarian Song

Moderatamente mosso (♩ = 116)

Traditional
Arr.: Rainer Mohrs

Track 59/60 Itchy Feet

Country Rock

G. K.

D Piano part

Track 61/62 O How Fleeting, O How Paltry

Melchior Franck
(1580–1639)
Arr.: G. K.

D Piano part

Maestoso

Theme from Duet Opus 2, No. 8

Joseph Reinagle
(1762–1836)

From: J. Reinagle, Easy Cello Duets Op. 2, Schott CB 250

Track 63/64 Jam Track 3: Funky Time

G. K.

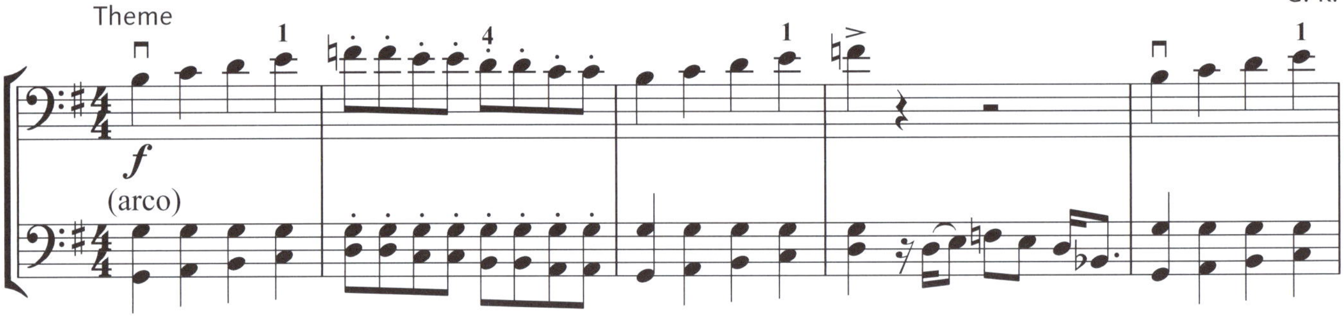

Fine

Improvise with the G minor pentatonic scale

Solo section 16 measures (bars)

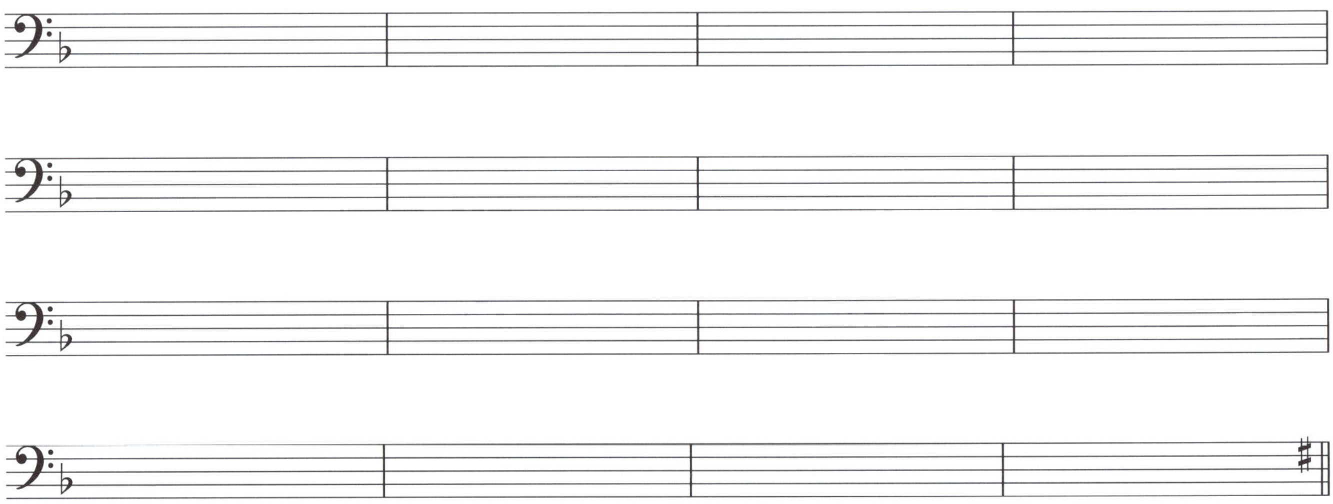

D. C. al Fine

Accompaniment to solo section:

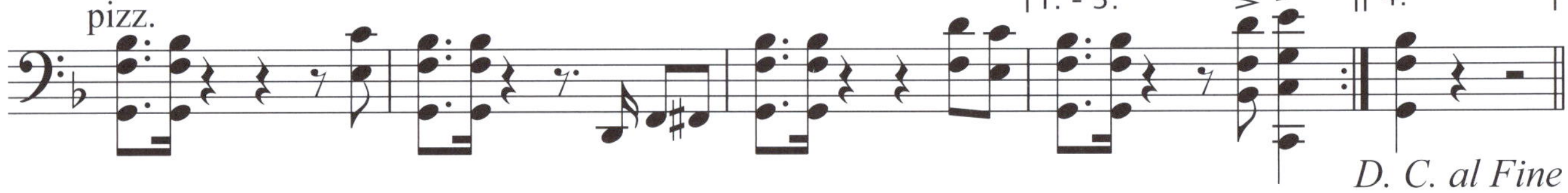

D. C. al Fine

Piano part
sample solo on audio-track

Cantabile

Bernhard Romberg
(1767–1841)

Find more lovely duos in 'Duets For Fun' by Elmar Preusser, Schott ED 13885

Track 65/66

Roller Coaster Polka

G. K.

Syncopation

In 4/4 time the accents usually fall on the 1st and 3rd beats:

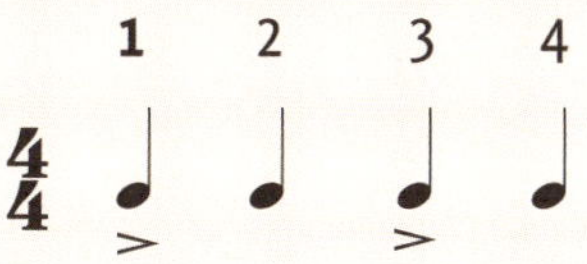

But if you merge an accented note with the unaccented note before it, the original accent is 'swallowed' by the preceding note and the accent is shifted forwards.

Here the 3rd beat is 'swallowed' by the 2nd:

is the same as

and here the 1st beat is 'swallowed' by the 4th:

Syncopation:
Anticipating (bringing forward) a note so the accent shifts onto a previously unaccented beat.

Play:

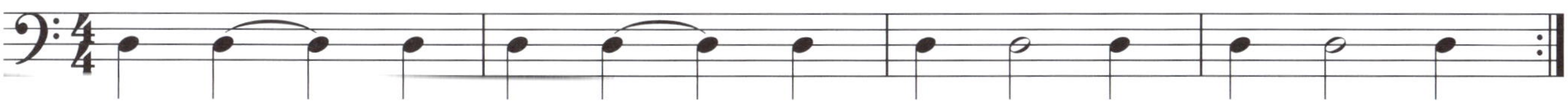

Time for Rag

G. K.

Track 67/68 Syncopation Blues

G. K.

D Piano part

With these notes (C minor pentatonic scale) you can improvise to the playback track:

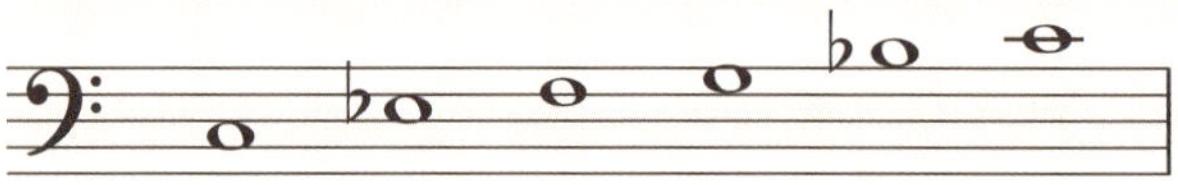

Canon

Georg Philipp Telemann
(1681–1767)

Track 69/70 Somebody's Knockin' At Your Door

Spiritual
Arr.: G. K.

acc. = accelerando = getting faster

D Piano part

Write out 'Somebody's Knockin' At Your Door' at double tempo:

Charleston Time

G. K.

Charleston:
a dance in 4/4 time popular in the USA in the 1920s

Track 71/72 Nobody Knows The Trouble I've Seen

Spiritual
Arr.: G. K.

D.C. al Fine

Track 73/74 New Shoe Rag

G. K.

From: G. Koeppen, 'Position Fun', Schott ED 21396

Go Down Moses

Spiritual
Arr: G. K.

Bowings and variants for scales

Bowings for broken chords

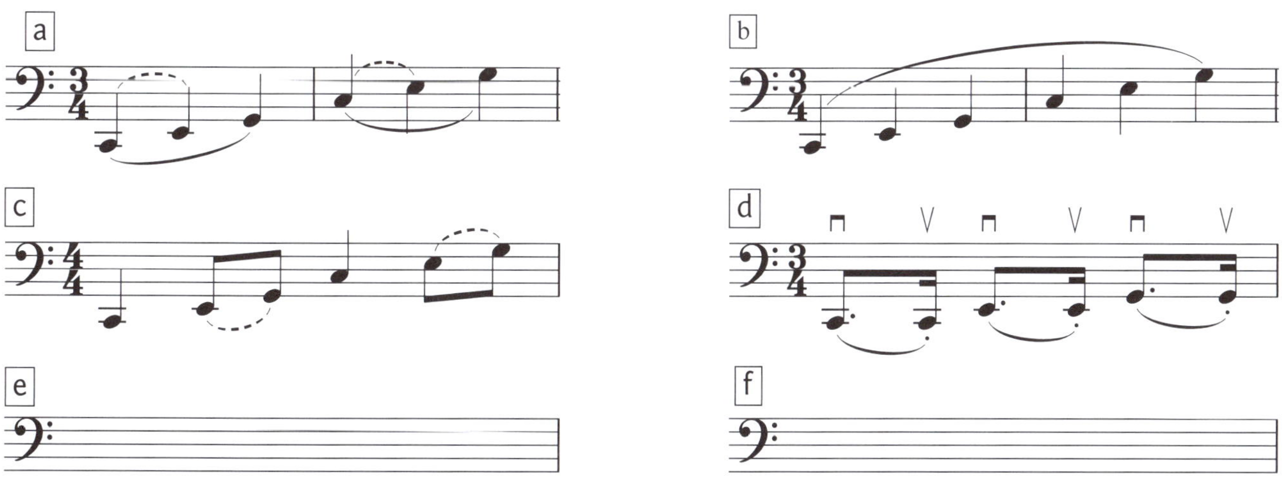

Manuscript paper for writing your own notes

Tracklist

Track	title
1/2	Tomorrow Morning
3/4	*Branle*
5/6	Long, Long Ago
7/8	Dance Tune
9/10	Rodeo
11/12	Rockin' Bass
13/14	Old Brass Wagon
15/16	Breakout
17/18	Skip To My Lou
19	Jam track 1: Meditation
20/21	*Alouette*
22/23	*Allemande*
24/25	Reggae
26/27	A Pleasant Ride
28/29	*Contredanse*
30/31	Strolling Along
32/33	Yankee Doodle
34/35	If You're Happy And You Know It
36/37	Fate
38/39	Skye Boat Song
40/41	Jazzy Tarantella
42/43	Greensleeves
44	Playing by ear 1
45	Playing by ear 2
46	Jam track 2: Billy's Rock
47/48	Rock It!
49/50	Sunbathing
51/52	Hangover on the Don
53/54	Market Day
55/56	Triplet Mood
57/58	Amazing Grace
59/60	Itchy Feet
61/62	O How Fleeting
63/64	Jam track 3: Funky Time
65/66	Roller Coaster Polka
67/68	Syncopation Blues
69/70	Somebody's Knockin' At Your Door
71/72	Nobody Knows The Trouble I've Seen
73/74	New Shoe Rag
75	Tuning note A (441 Hertz)
76	Tuning note D
77	Tuning note G
78	Tuning note C

The second number relates to the play-along version (half playback).